Original title:
Follow Your Heart

Copyright © 2024 Creative Arts Management OÜ
All rights reserved.

Author: Clement Portlander
ISBN HARDBACK: 978-9916-88-038-8
ISBN PAPERBACK: 978-9916-88-039-5

Navigating Through Moonlit Haze

Beneath the silver glow we roam,
Whispers of shadows lead us home.
Stars above like diamonds shine,
Guiding hearts that intertwine.

The path unfolds in softest light,
Painting dreams throughout the night.
Waves of mist, a gentle breath,
While silence hums a tune of depth.

With every step, the world holds still,
Feeling lost yet finding will.
Footfalls dance on hidden ground,
In this haze, true peace is found.

Secrets Beneath the Surface

In shadowed depths where secrets dwell,
A tale unfolds, too deep to tell.
Rippling waters, a whispered sound,
Mysteries lost but never found.

Beneath the calm, a tempest churns,
As stillness masks what often burns.
The heart remembers every ache,
In silence, all the truths we break.

Glistening scales, both sharp and fine,
Guarding stories, a sacred line.
Dive below where dreams are spun,
And face the fight that can't be won.

The Road Less Tread

Winding paths through thickened brush,
Options fade in twilight's hush.
Footprints fade in dust and grass,
But where they lead, I'll surely pass.

The air is thick with whispered lore,
Echoes of those who ventured before.
Courage swells with every stride,
In this choice, I choose to glide.

Sunlight filters through the trees,
Stirring hopes like a gentle breeze.
Nothing holds as I explore,
The less traveled, I adore.

A Symphony of Inner Echoes

In chambers deep where silence dwells,
A song emerges, time repels.
Whispers of dreams, a haunting tune,
Breathe life beneath the silver moon.

Resonance of thoughts, pure and bright,
Guiding shadows into the light.
Each heartbeat sings a sweet refrain,
Melodies that dance through pain.

The symphony of past and now,
Plays softly on a woven bow.
In every note, a story weaves,
Through echoes, my spirit believes.

Sailing into Tomorrow

On waves that whisper dreams anew,
We sail beneath the sky so blue.
With wind as guide, our hopes take flight,
Towards the dawn, into the light.

Each swell a promise, each breeze a chance,
We navigate life's shifting dance.
In the horizon's glow, we find our way,
To brighter shores, where we shall stay.

The Pulse of Adventure

In the heart of the wild, a call rings clear,
With every step, we cast off fear.
Mountains rise like bold, fierce dreams,
Where nothing's ever as it seems.

The rivers sing, the forests play,
In nature's arms, we lose our way.
With dreams as anchors, we boldly roam,
Finding in the wild, a sense of home.

Quest for the Unseen

Beneath the stars, we chase the night,
In shadows deep, we seek the light.
Whispers of fate in the silent air,
Guide us onward with gentle care.

Through veils of mist, we wander far,
In search of truths, like hidden stars.
Every step leads to worlds unknown,
In the quest for the unseen, we've grown.

Echoes in the Wilderness

Through tangled woods, the echoes play,
They carry stories of yesterday.
The rustling leaves, a soft refrain,
In wilderness, we hear the pain.

As mountains stand with timeless grace,
We find our voice, a sacred space.
In the silence loud, where we belong,
The echoes guide us, fierce and strong.

Journeying Through the Unknown

With footsteps silent in the night,
I wander paths obscured from sight.
The stars map dreams in twilight's glow,
Each breath a promise, hearts in tow.

Through shadows deep and whispers rare,
I chase the echoes, heed the flare.
What lies beyond the horizon's fold?
A future shimmering, bright and bold.

Threads of the Unfathomable

In every thread the stories weave,
Mysteries spun, we dare believe.
Tangled destinies in the dark,
Each stitch a path, each knot a spark.

The fabric holds the tales untold,
Of hearts entwined and dreams of gold.
We grasp for truth in tangled seams,
Finding solace in woven dreams.

The Pulse of Possibility

In the stillness, a heartbeat hums,
A rhythm soft, where potential comes.
Each heartbeat whispers, 'You can be,'
The pulse of life, unbound and free.

With every step, the world unfolds,
A canvas bright, with tales of old.
What if, what could, the endless game,
In the dance of time, we stake our claim.

Dance of the Undaunted

The brave take flight on winds of chance,
With hearts ablaze, they choose to dance.
Through storms and trials, they stand tall,
   Resilient echoes, answering the call.

   With every leap, they shatter fears,
  In the rhythm, they embrace the years.
  Together bound, in courage's light,
The dance of the undaunted takes its flight.

The Invitation of Tomorrow

Awake with the dawn, a whisper calls,
Echoes of dreams in the golden halls.
The sun paints the sky with colors so bright,
Offering hope in the soft morning light.

Step forward with courage, let shadows fade,
In the arms of the future, new paths are laid.
Every heartbeat sings a soft tune of grace,
Inviting you gently to take your place.

The Heart's Quiet Revolution

In silence it stirs, a soft surge of flame,
Breaking the bonds that once felt like a game.
Whispers of change dance through the air,
Filling the spaces with tender care.

Moments unravel, the past slips away,
New rhythms of life begin to sway.
A pulse of softness, a strength found anew,
The heart beats in time with a vision so true.

A Voyage of Self-Discovery

Set sail on the seas of uncharted thought,
With each wave you ride, new lessons are brought.
The map of your soul unfolds with each tide,
In the depths of your heart, pure treasures reside.

Lost in the currents, find strength in the flow,
Every inch of the journey teaches you so.
Navigate stars that whisper your name,
And light up the skies with your vibrant flame.

Beneath the Surface of Dreams

In twilight's embrace, dreams weave and blend,
A tapestry rich where realities bend.
In shadows they flutter, like whispers of night,
Painting the darkness with luminous light.

Dive deep in the waters where visions reside,
The pulse of the depths becomes your guide.
Each ripple reveals what the heart longs to see,
In the stillness of night, you are truly free.

Heartbeats on the Move

Rhythms dance in twilight's glow,
Feet unbound, where wild winds blow.
Every step a story told,
In the night, brave hearts unfold.

Dreams like stars across the sky,
Chasing whispers, flying high.
Alive in moments, pulse in sync,
Heartbeats quicken, thoughts on brink.

Together under moonlit beams,
Wandering through our quiet dreams.
With every laugh, our spirits soar,
The journey calls, let's seek for more.

The Unwritten Chapters of Desire

Ink yet wet upon the page,
Heartfelt words begin to rage.
In each silence, stories wait,
Unfolding slowly, hearts create.

Like gentle waves upon the shore,
Whispers echo, longing more.
Pages turning, fate in hand,
Shadows dancing on soft sand.

Every glance, a secret penned,
Threads of longing never end.
Chapters woven, hopes entwined,
In the depths, our souls aligned.

Whispering Desires

Soft murmurs in the night,
Hearts aflame, dreams take flight.
With every breath, a wish is spun,
Lost in shadows, we are one.

Gentle sighs as time moves slow,
In the twilight, secrets grow.
Dreams unfurl like petals wide,
In this space, we will abide.

Each heartbeat echoes soft and clear,
A melody of hope and fear.
In the hush, we dare to feel,
Whispered truths that softly heal.

The Compass Within

Guiding stars light up the night,
In our hearts, purest light.
A flame that flickers, strong yet sweet,
Leading us where worlds may meet.

Maps unseen, yet paths unfold,
Stories born, waiting bold.
In each moment, choices lie,
Follow dreams or let wind fly.

The compass whispers, trust your soul,
In the journey, find the whole.
Hearts will guide us through the fray,
The compass leads, come what may.

Navigating by Starlight

Under the blanket of the night,
Stars whisper secrets, glowing bright.
The moon guides paths in silver hues,
As dreams take flight, we chase the muse.

Waves of silver paint the sea,
In silence, we learn to be free.
Each constellation, a guiding spark,
Illuminates our journey, though dark.

With every heartbeat, the cosmos sings,
We dance with hope, on stardust wings.
Navigating through the vast unknown,
Our spirits soar, no longer alone.

In the embrace of night's calm air,
We find our way, without a care.
The starlight beckons, soft and clear,
In its glow, we shed our fear.

The Symphony of Your Spirit

In the silence, your essence flows,
A melody only the heart knows.
Each note a whisper, rich and true,
Crafting a symphony just for you.

The rhythm of life dances along,
A heartbeat echoing a joyful song.
With every pulse, emotions rise,
Harmonies bloom, like stars in the skies.

In this concert of soul's delight,
Every fear fades into the night.
As laughter rings, and tears take flight,
Your spirit shines, a beacon of light.

Together we weave this timeless art,
A grand crescendo, soul to heart.
In the symphony, we find our way,
Creating music that forever will stay.

Courageous Heartbeats

In the stillness, courage stirs,
Echoes of strength in whispered purrs.
Each heartbeat, a vow we make,
Against the odds, we rise, not break.

Through storms that shake, and winds that howl,
We find our fire, fierce and foul.
With every breath, we push ahead,
Embracing paths where fears have led.

Together, we forge our own way,
With each brave choice, we seize the day.
A tapestry woven with threads of hope,
In unity, we learn to cope.

Our heartbeat echoes with love's fierce song,
In the face of darkness, we belong.
With courage alight in every heart,
Together we rise; we'll never part.

The Journey of True Belonging

In the quiet corners of our hearts,
We seek connections, where love starts.
Each smile a bridge, each laugh a key,
Unlocking doors to what can be.

Through valleys low and mountains high,
We wander, searching for the why.
In every face, a mirrored soul,
Finding pieces that make us whole.

Every shared story, a thread so fine,
Weaving a tapestry, yours and mine.
From distant shores to familiar lands,
In unity, our journey stands.

Together we write our history,
In every moment, a victory.
True belonging, a treasure sought,
In love and friendship, we find what's bought.

Reaching for the Shimmering Stars

In the depth of night, we gaze,
Hopes afloat in gentle rays.
Whispers from a distant sphere,
Every twinkle draws us near.

Dreams like comets, swift and wild,
Each a secret, every child.
Guiding lights, with stories told,
The universe, a treasure, gold.

Eyes ablaze with cosmic fire,
Yearning souls, we never tire.
Hands outstretched, we seek to soar,
To the heavens, forevermore.

A celestial dance begins anew,
With every wish that we pursue.
In the silence, stars align,
Reaching forth, our hearts divine.

In Harmony with Wonders

Nature sings a sweet refrain,
Every note, a soft embrace.
Mountains rise and rivers play,
In this world, we find our way.

Leaves that flutter in the breeze,
Whisper secrets through the trees.
Colors blend, a vibrant show,
In this dance, we come to know.

Harmony in every sound,
Life's pure beauty all around.
Side by side, we walk the path,
In stillness, feel the aftermath.

Together, hearts and minds unite,
In the glow of shared delight.
With the wonders all around,
We find peace, where love is found.

A Journey Beyond Comfort

Stepping forth from cozy nests,
Into lands where courage tests.
Facing fears, we push the lines,
In the unknown, our spirit shines.

Roads less traveled call our name,
Adventurous hearts, we still aim.
With each stride, we shed the doubt,
In discomfort, we learn what's out.

Mountains high, the valleys deep,
Through the trials, our dreams we keep.
Every moment, choice to grow,
In discomfort, we learn to glow.

Transforming pain to strength we find,
The journey shapes our hearts and mind.
Being brave in paths unplanned,
Is where life's true magic stands.

The Map of Uncharted Joy

On pages blank, we sketch the lines,
With dreams that sparkle, bright as signs.
Every adventure yet to start,
Holds the secrets of the heart.

With each step, a story grows,
In laughter's echo, love still flows.
Wonders wait at every turn,
In our souls, a fire burns.

Guided by our hopes and dreams,
Life unfolds in joyful streams.
Through unmarked trails, we navigate,
Finding joy in every fate.

A treasure map of heart's delight,
Leading us through day and night.
In the canvas of our days,
We discover joy's sweet ways.

A Quest for Soul's Companion

In shadows deep, I search for light,
A whisper soft, to guide my flight.
Through ancient woods where secrets lie,
A heart that beats beneath the sky.

With every step, the path unfolds,
In quiet dreams, a hand I hold.
Together bound by fate's design,
A companion true, our spirits align.

The stars above, they seem to wink,
In moments shared, we start to think.
Of journeys long, of tales untold,
In love's embrace, our hands grow bold.

So onward tread, this quest in heart,
For in this life, we play our part.
In each connection, find our role,
In every touch, a quest for soul.

Moments Whispered in Solitude

In silence deep, the thoughts arise,
A gentle breeze, the unseen sighs.
Reflection glows like morning dew,
In solitude, I dance with you.

With every breath, a moment sways,
In quiet corners, where the heart stays.
An echo soft, a still embrace,
In sacred time, I find my place.

The shadows speak in whispered tones,
As solitude reveals its stones.
Through quiet nights, the candles glow,
In fragile peace, I come to know.

These whispered gifts, in stillness found,
In solitude, my soul unbound.
With every heartbeat, shadows clear,
Moments cherished, always near.

The Unseen Threads Weave

Through silent hands, the threads align,
In shadows cast, our fates entwine.
The fabric thick with dreams and hopes,
Weaving life's intricate scopes.

From distant lands, to moments shared,
Among the lost, the hopeful dared.
In every knot, a story spun,
A tapestry where all is one.

The unseen hands that pull and bind,
In every heart, a love defined.
Through laughter, tears, the fibers grow,
In every breath, the truths we sow.

As strands intertwine, we come to see,
The beauty in this grand decree.
For in each thread, a tale carved deep,
In woven dreams, our souls we keep.

Paths Culled from Gut Feelings

In whispers low, intuition calls,
Through winding paths, where shadows fall.
A gut instinct, a hidden guide,
Through tangled woods, I will abide.

With open heart, I walk the line,
In every step, a truth divine.
The whispers lead through thick and thin,
Each fork a chance, a place to begin.

Through choices made, the journey bends,
In every turn, the spirit mends.
These paths we walk, though not in sight,
Are filled with grace, and endless light.

So trust the whispers, heed the call,
For gut feelings guide us through it all.
In every stumble, rise anew,
The paths we choose are dreams that grew.

Chasing Whispers of the Soul

In the silence, whispers glide,
Echoes of dreams, side by side.
Mysteries weave through the night,
Guiding the heart, shining bright.

Stars above twinkle and sway,
Tales of old in soft array.
Each heartbeat, a hidden song,
Leading us where we belong.

Gentle winds carry the sound,
Secrets of love all around.
Chasing shadows, we shall roam,
Finding the path to our home.

Through the dark, we seek the light,
Whispers guiding, hearts take flight.
In the dance of soul's allure,
We chase the whispers, pure and sure.

Unraveled Paths of Desire

In the garden of yearning hearts,
Desires bloom, play various parts.
Paths entwined like tangled vines,
Secrets held in thin designs.

Underneath the moon's soft gaze,
We navigate through passion's maze.
Each twist and turn, a new embrace,
Unraveled dreams, we boldly chase.

Treading lightly, fears aside,
With courage, souls open wide.
In the echo of hopes untold,
Unraveled paths, brave and bold.

Journeying through the night's embrace,
Every moment, a sacred space.
Desires whisper, softly conspire,
Together we ignite the fire.

Dancing with Inner Compass

The heart beats to its own sweet tune,
A rhythm that hums beneath the moon.
With each step, we find our way,
Dancing free, come what may.

Guided by the stars so bright,
Navigating through the night.
Whispers of the soul do sing,
In this dance, we find our wings.

Twists and turns with every beat,
Aligning our steps, feeling complete.
With trust in our inner guide,
We dance boldly, hearts open wide.

Each movement, a story told,
In the rhythm, we are bold.
Dancing with our compass true,
Finding paths that lead to you.

A Journey of Hidden Wishes

In the quiet of the night,
Whispers of wishes take their flight.
Each one wrapped in a secret sigh,
Yearning to soar, reaching high.

Along the road of dreams untold,
Hidden treasures, bright and bold.
With every step, we venture far,
Guided by our own North Star.

In the shadows, wishes gleam,
Flickering softly like a dream.
Together, we collect the light,
Embracing hope, dispelling fright.

A journey paved with stars anew,
Hidden wishes shine right through.
With each heartbeat, we explore,
Unlocking dreams forevermore.

A Tapestry of Wishes

In twilight glow, dreams softly weave,
Threads of hope, in hearts believe.
Whispers dance on the gentle breeze,
Carrying wishes, bringing ease.

Stars above, in the velvet night,
Guide our paths, igniting light.
In every stitch, a story spun,
A tapestry of what's to come.

With each breath, new hopes arise,
Painting futures beneath the skies.
Together, we'll chase the gleams,
Uniting the fabric of our dreams.

From distant shores to mountains high,
Wishes soar, like birds in the sky.
A woven tale of love and grace,
In this tapestry, we find our place.

The Call of Serenity

In quiet woods where whispers blend,
Nature's voice, a soothing friend.
Rivers murmur, trees stand tall,
In this haven, we hear the call.

Softly now, the shadows play,
As sunlight weaves a golden ray.
The waters speak, inviting rest,
In serenity, we feel the best.

A gentle breeze, a moment's pause,
Life's symphony, without a cause.
With every breath, the burdens cease,
In this sanctuary, we find peace.

Close your eyes, let worries fade,
In this calm, dreams are made.
Embrace the stillness, let it flow,
For in serenity, we truly grow.

In Search of Beliefs

Upon the path where questions lie,
We seek the truth, we reach for the sky.
Every step, a quest profound,
In shadows deep, our doubts abound.

With open hearts, we bravely roam,
Searching for meaning, finding home.
In every story, a lesson learned,
In the fires of faith, our spirits burned.

Through whispered doubts and echoes loud,
We rise again, we stand proud.
In every soul, a flicker bright,
Together we shine, chasing the light.

To find beliefs that nourish and grow,
In every pulse, let wisdom flow.
Together we weave our tapestry,
In search of truths to set us free.

Navigating Life's Currents

In flowing streams, life's river glides,
With twists and turns, where fate abides.
We sail our boats through calm and storm,
Finding strength in every form.

Waves may crash and winds may howl,
But through it all, we'll not convolve.
With sails unfurled, we chase the day,
Navigating dreams, come what may.

Every dawn, a chance to steer,
With courage strong, we conquer fear.
In each heartbeat, the compass aligns,
Guiding us through, as life entwines.

So let us journey, hand in hand,
Across the seas, to distant lands.
For in this voyage, we'll find our way,
Navigating life, come what may.

Embrace the Winds of Change

The winds arrive, a gentle sigh,
Whispering secrets as they fly.
Leaves twist and dance with grace anew,
A promise of life, the old made true.

Seasons shift, the canvas shifts,
Colors burst, the heart uplifts.
Each moment sways, a fleeting glance,
Embrace the winds, take a chance.

Clouds may gather, shadows fall,
Yet light breaks forth, answering the call.
Through storms we grow, through trials, we thrive,
In every change, we come alive.

So let your spirit soar and bend,
As the winds of change become your friend.
A journey awaits, so wild and wide,
Embrace the winds, let them be your guide.

The Pathway of Intent

Footsteps carved on sacred ground,
With every choice, a voice resounds.
Hearts aligned with purpose clear,
The pathway beckons, drawing near.

Intent shines bright, a guiding light,
In the morning's soft, golden bright.
Dreams take form, as we tread on,
With every sunrise, a new bond drawn.

Step by step, with courage we rise,
Minds awakened, opening our eyes.
Wander through the woods of the heart,
On this journey, we play our part.

So walk the path, with love's finesse,
Each intention drives the quest.
For every step, a world to see,
On the pathway of intent, we're free.

In Tune with the Soul's Muse

A melody hums in the quiet night,
Bringing forth dreams, pure and bright.
Colors of thought weave through the dark,
In tune with the soul, we find our spark.

Brush of a breeze, whispers on skin,
In the heart of the stillness, creativity begins.
Each note, a wave that ebbs and flows,
In the dance of inspiration, the spirit knows.

Lines of history etched in the mind,
Story and rhythm, beautifully aligned.
Artistry whispered from deep within,
In tune with our muse, we learn to begin.

So listen closely, let the heart soar,
For the soul's muse knocks, inviting more.
With each creation, we take our flight,
In tune with the muse, we embrace the light.

Light in the Depths

In shadowed valleys, darkness may creep,
Yet within the silence, the light does seep.
Glimmers of hope in the coldest night,
Shine ever bright, a powerful sight.

Through the murk, we learn to see,
The beauty lies in humility.
A flicker of warmth in the depths does flow,
Guiding the heart to where it may grow.

Lost in the depths, yet finding our way,
The heart ignites, as night turns to day.
For every struggle, a lesson unfolds,
In the light of the depths, true strength beholds.

So fear not the dark, embrace its grace,
For the light will always find a place.
In the depths we dance, with fire and calm,
For within our hearts, there lies the balm.

A Promise of Tomorrow

In the dawn's first light we stand,
Whispers of hope held in our hands.
Together we'll chase the fleeting dream,
Building a future like a sunlit stream.

With every step, we rise and soar,
The past behind, we seek the shore.
Clouds may gather, storms may rage,
But love will guide us through each page.

A promise made, sweet and clear,
In these moments, we hold dear.
As stars align, our paths entwine,
Tomorrow's light forever shines.

The Heart's Gentle Whisper

In silence deep, a truth unfolds,
A tender touch, a story told.
Amidst the chaos, a calm resides,
The heart's soft whispers, where love abides.

With every beat, a message sent,
In passion's glow, our souls are lent.
Through quiet moments, we gently find,
The beauty of two hearts unconfined.

An echo found in starlit skies,
In every glance, a sweet surprise.
The heart knows secrets, soft and bright,
Guiding us through the darkest night.

Dancing to the Beat of Desire

Under moonlit skies, we sway as one,
Rhythms pulse, our hearts outrun.
In the embrace of night's sweet grace,
We lose ourselves in love's warm space.

Each step we take, a spark ignites,
In the heat of passion, we claim our rights.
With every twirl, our spirits rise,
Dancing freely beneath the skies.

Fingers entwined, we share the beat,
In this melody, our souls meet.
Let the world fade, we are alive,
In the dance of love, together we thrive.

Uncharted Destinies

With every sunrise, paths unfold,
Mysteries wrapped, stories untold.
Together we wander, hand in hand,
Exploring a world, vast and grand.

The winds of change, they softly blow,
Guiding our hearts where we don't know.
With courage found in each new chance,
Life's canvas waits for our bold dance.

In uncharted lands, we find our way,
Bright tomorrow awaits today.
Together we forge, against the tide,
In the journey of life, love will abide.

Wherever the Wind May Carry

In the sky where the eagles soar,
Whispers of freedom forevermore.
Through valleys deep and mountains high,
The wind calls softly, hear its sigh.

Across the plains where wildflowers bloom,
It dances lightly, dispelling gloom.
With every tune, it carries dreams,
A gentle force that flows and beams.

From distant shores to forest glades,
It weaves through shadows and glinting blades.
Wherever it leads, I will follow true,
For the spirit of nature calls anew.

Embrace the journey and let it flow,
As the wind reveals what we must know.
With open hearts, we journey wide,
Wherever the wind may choose to guide.

The Silent Guide of Intuition

In the stillness of the night,
A voice emerges, soft and light.
It whispers gently, calm and clear,
Trust its wisdom, hold it near.

When shadows linger, doubts arise,
The heart's true compass never lies.
A guiding star in the darkest hour,
Intuition blooms, a hidden flower.

Follow the pulse that lies within,
It leads you forth, where dreams begin.
In silence, find the crystal truth,
To nurture hope and spark your youth.

With every step, the path unfolds,
Listen closely to what it holds.
In this journey, trust and see,
The silent guide will set you free.

Dreams Carved in Starlight

In the twilight's gentle grace,
Dreams awaken, find their place.
Beneath the vast celestial dome,
Whispers of wishes feel like home.

Each twinkle holds a story bright,
Carved in starlight, shimmering light.
The moonlight paints the night's embrace,
As dreams begin to intertwine and lace.

With each heartbeat, visions bloom,
A tapestry in the night's cool loom.
Stars wink secrets, softly they share,
A world of wonders awaiting our care.

Catch the flicker of your heart's delight,
In the stillness, find your flight.
For in starlight, dreams reside,
A universe where hopes abide.

Embracing the Inner Fire

In the heart where passion burns,
A flame ignites, as spirit yearns.
With every spark, a story grows,
A vibrant force that brightly glows.

Through trials faced and shadows cast,
The inner fire will hold steadfast.
It fuels the journey, fierce and true,
A beacon shining just for you.

With open arms, embrace the heat,
Let it guide you, feel the beat.
From ember small to blazing height,
Awaken dreams and take to flight.

Stand strong and face the winds of change,
Embrace the fire, let it range.
For inside you lies endless power,
Blooming bright like a radiant flower.

Chasing the Echo of Hope

In the shadows, whispers linger,
Dreams take flight on silver wings,
Hearts will search for brighter mornings,
Each step brings new beginnings.

Through the valleys, through the night,
Faith will guide the weary soul,
With each dawn, a spark ignites,
Hope, our ever-present goal.

Every tear falls like a raindrop,
Washing pain from weary eyes,
In the distance, echoes call,
A promise heard beneath the skies.

Chasing echoes, we find strength,
With each heartbeat, courage grows,
Together, we will rise at length,
On this path, the future glows.

The Road Less Traveled

A path that's bent, a route unknown,
Where wildflowers dance and sway,
With every choice, a seed is sown,
Onward, onward, come what may.

The woods remain a mystery,
With whispers hiding at each turn,
In silence, strength will set us free,
And in the dark, our spirits burn.

Every footstep leaves a mark,
In stories waiting to unfold,
With dreams igniting from the spark,
A journey marked with tales untold.

So take a breath, embrace the climb,
Let courage guide you through the night,
For on this road, we find our rhyme,
In every shadow, there's a light.

Where Passion Leads

In the heart's deep, burning core,
A flame ignites with vibrant hue,
Chasing visions, longing for more,
Embracing everything that's true.

Each brushstroke paints a vibrant dream,
Where colors blend and voices soar,
In whispered hopes, the glimmers beam,
With every heartbeat, we explore.

Through the storm and through the fire,
We rise and fall, we break and mend,
With every pulse, we dare aspire,
Together forged, with love, we blend.

So let your spirit boldly fly,
Beyond the confines of the day,
For where passion leads, we won't deny,
A world awaits — come take your way.

The Rhythm of Your Longing

In the silence, hear the pulse,
A heartbeat echoing your dreams,
Through shadows deep, where visions waltz,
Feel the pull of unseen streams.

Every wish a tender note,
Every sigh a whispered tune,
In the distance, hearts will float,
Dancing 'neath the silver moon.

Let the rhythm guide your feet,
As you sway to the unspoken,
In the melody, passion meets,
A promise forged, never broken.

With each breath, the longing grows,
In the cadence of the night,
Follow where your spirit flows,
In this dance, you find your light.

Following the Footsteps of Serendipity

In fleeting moments, chance does play,
Paths intertwine, come what may.
Whispers of fate, a gentle tease,
Serendipity dances on the breeze.

We wander through the unknown light,
Guided by dreams that take to flight.
Hands reaching out for the unseen,
In this tapestry, we weave our sheen.

With laughter echoing through the night,
Each step taken brings new delight.
The world unfolds, a grand surprise,
In serendipity, our spirit flies.

So trust the journey, let it flow,
For magic thrives when hearts aglow.
In paths uncharted, we find our way,
Through whispers of fate, we choose to stay.

The Harmonies of Desire

In our hearts, a music plays,
A symphony of longing stays.
Each note whispers, sweet and low,
As tides of passion rise and flow.

With every glance, a spark ignites,
In shadows deep, where love invites.
Desire dances, wild and free,
In perfect rhythms, you and me.

We weave a melody of grace,
In tender moments, we embrace.
The chords of yearning fill the air,
In harmonies, we cast our care.

So let us sing the song of dreams,
Through vibrant hues and soft moonbeams.
In the serenade of hearts aflame,
Desire guides us, calls our name.

A Journey to the Soul's Depth

In silence profound, we take the dive,
Exploring realms where spirits thrive.
Beneath the surface, truths reside,
In depths of soul where hopes abide.

With every breath, we seek to know,
The secrets buried deep below.
Visions whisper, soft and wise,
In shadows cast, the spirit flies.

Through trials faced and lessons learned,
We find the flame that brightly burned.
With open hearts, we tread the path,
Embracing light as shadows pass.

In every heartbeat, wisdom grows,
In sacred spaces, love bestows.
A journey deep, to self we rise,
In the soul's depth, the truth belies.

Echoes of Truth

In whispers soft, the truth reveals,
Each echo carries how it feels.
Resounding deep, in heart and mind,
A tapestry of thoughts entwined.

The past resounds in every phrase,
In echoes long, our spirit stays.
Time bends close, where memories play,
In every turn, the truth will sway.

Though shadows loom and doubts arise,
The light of truth will never disguise.
It stands as guide through every plight,
A beacon bold in endless night.

So listen close, and you shall find,
The echoes of the heart aligned.
In every moment, hear the call,
For truth resounds, it claims us all.

Compass of the Unheard

In shadows deep, the whispers lie,
Silent paths where secrets sigh.
A compass points to dreams untold,
Searching for truths in the cold.

Lost in echoes of the night,
Hear the call, feel the light.
Invisible maps guide us through,
To places known but never true.

Voices dance on the edges near,
Yearning for hearts that want to hear.
A journey sought, yet never planned,
In the silence we make our stand.

Crimson skies and starlit seas,
Navigate the gentle breeze.
With each step we're finally free,
Guided by what cannot be.

The Language of Yearning

Words unspoken flutter close,
In quiet hearts, it softly grows.
Each glance a poem, each sigh a song,
In the stillness, where we belong.

Longing whispers through the air,
A melody we both can share.
Every heartbeat writes a line,
In a language both yours and mine.

Time stands still in moments brief,
Yet covers all like falling leaf.
Silently, dreams intertwine,
In shadows of a love divine.

With every breath, our hopes take flight,
Leaving trails of purest light.
In every pause, a world appears,
A testament to all our years.

Serendipity's Gentle Push

Across the path, fate softly plays,
In unexpected, winding ways.
A chance encounter, laughter shared,
In fleeting moments, love is bared.

Gentle nudges from the stars,
Leading us to heal the scars.
In every twist, a spark ignites,
Guiding hearts through darkened nights.

With open hearts, we walk the line,
Trusting that the world will shine.
Each stumble feels like a dance,
In serendipity's sweet chance.

Threads of fate start to entwine,
Drawing close what fate designs.
In the chaos, beauty rests,
Finding joy in all the quests.

Windswept Journeys of the Heart

Through valleys low and mountains high,
With dreams that soar, like birds on high.
Each journey carved by love's embrace,
Windswept whispers in a sacred space.

With every step, the heart takes flight,
Guided by stars in the velvet night.
A tale of trials, laughter, tears,
Echoing through the distant years.

As the winds change, so does the soul,
Finding solace in the whole.
In the wild, we learn to roam,
Each heartbeat shapes a place called home.

Embrace the storms, the calm, the sun,
For each journey is a race just begun.
Together we'll write the lines of art,
Windswept journeys, of the heart.

The Call of Wildflowers

In fields of gold and violet hues,
Beneath the sun, where beauty brews.
They sway and dance, rejoice in light,
A whisper to the heart takes flight.

With petals soft, their fragrance sweet,
They beckon souls, a gentle greet.
In every shade and every bloom,
They paint the world, dispel the gloom.

Each blossom tells a tale untold,
Of summer days and nights so bold.
In nature's hand, they find their place,
A fleeting glimpse of purest grace.

So wander forth, let wildflowers guide,
Through meadows wide, with hearts open wide.
Each step a song, each sight a cheer,
In the call of flowers, love draws near.

The Canvas of Your Yearning

Your heart a canvas, blank and bright,
Awaiting strokes of day and night.
With dreams as colors, bold and deep,
You paint the visions that you keep.

Tread softly now, with brush in hand,
Each thought a mark on shifting sand.
Emotions swirl, they blend and flow,
Creating worlds that ebb and glow.

With every heartbeat, every sigh,
The hues of hope will never die.
In shadows cast, in light so clear,
The canvas sings what you hold dear.

So let your spirit rise and soar,
Embrace the art, unlock the door.
For in each stroke, your truth will shine,
A masterpiece that's truly mine.

Harmony of the Seekers

In twilight's hush, we find our way,
Where whispers weave through dusk and day.
With wandering hearts, we seek the light,
In harmony, we take our flight.

Each step a song of dreams unfurled,
Together, we explore the world.
Through mountains high and valleys low,
Our spirits dance, our visions grow.

With open arms and minds so free,
In every moment, we shall see.
The beauty wrapped in nature's grace,
A bond of love we can't erase.

So hand in hand, we journey on,
Through twilight's glow, and breaking dawn.
In harmony, we'll find our way,
Forever seekers, come what may.

The Heart's Odyssey

Upon the waves of time we sail,
Through storms and calm, we will not fail.
Each pulse a rhythm, every beat,
A journey paved with love so sweet.

In dreams we wander, far and wide,
With hopes as anchors, hearts as guide.
We chart the stars, the path unknown,
Together in this realm we've grown.

Through shadows cast and sunshine bright,
We navigate the depths of night.
Each lesson learned, a treasure found,
In every whisper, life profound.

So let us dance beneath the skies,
Embrace the wonders, cast our cries.
For every journey shapes our soul,
The heart's odyssey, forever whole.

Beyond the Boundaries of Fear

Step beyond the shadows cast,
Where dreams embrace the light,
Let courage break the chains,
And take your leap of flight.

Whispers of hope surround us,
In every gentle breeze,
With hearts ablaze with passion,
We'll rise above the seas.

The walls that held us captive,
Shall crumble with a roar,
For freedom's song is calling,
We'll dance forevermore.

So venture into the unknown,
Where fears begin to fade,
In every step, a victory,
A fearless path is made.

The Allure of Unwritten Pages

Inkless sheets before me lie,
A canvas for the heart,
Each line a chance to capture,
The stories yet to start.

Whispers of potential call,
In silence, dreams await,
The magic of the moment,
To craft and to create.

With every stroke and thought unfurled,
A universe resides,
Within the written wonders,
Where fantasy abides.

I'll weave my tale of laughter,
Of sorrow, love, and pain,
Beyond the ink and paper,
A world that has no chain.

When Wishes Take Flight

Close your eyes and make a wish,
Let dreams begin to soar,
With every hope that dances,
It opens up a door.

The sky is vast and endless,
Where wishes float like birds,
A symphony of laughter,
In whispers without words.

With wings of faith and purpose,
We'll chase the morning light,
For wishes held in heartbeats,
Are destined to ignite.

So let your spirit wander,
And set your dreams on fire,
For in the heart of wishing,
Lies every great desire.

Heartbeats Across the Horizon

In twilight's gentle embrace,
Our hearts begin to race,
With every pulse and echo,
We find our sacred place.

Across the vast horizon,
Two souls entwined as one,
With each beat harmonizing,
The journey's just begun.

With every shared intention,
We traverse lands unknown,
A tapestry of moments,
Together we have grown.

So let the world watch closely,
As heartbeats weave their song,
For love knows no boundaries,
In this we both belong.

Resounding Through the Silence

In the hush of twilight's grace,
Whispers roam the empty space.
Echoes of dreams softly call,
Carrying secrets, binding all.

Silent shadows start to weave,
Tales of hope, we long to believe.
In this calm, the heart can hear,
Truth unfurls, the path is clear.

Voices linger like a sigh,
Painting stars in the night sky.
In the stillness, love's refrain,
Breaks the quiet, eases pain.

Let us listen, hearts exposed,
In the silence, life's composed.
Resounding softly, ancient song,
In the stillness, we belong.

The Dance of Possibilities

These moments twirl like autumn leaves,
Carried by winds, each one deceives.
Paths unfold in vibrant streams,
Life ignites with vivid dreams.

Step by step, let courage rise,
Chasing visions through the skies.
Through the rhythm, we create,
A journey shared, a dance of fate.

In the circle, hearts unite,
Spinning dreams, embracing light.
Every chance a spark ignites,
In our souls, the future writes.

Fingers touched and laughter shared,
In this dance, we're truly dared.
The possible unfolds anew,
In each heartbeat, a chance to pursue.

Seeking the Soul's Radiance

In the depths where shadows creep,
Lies a light, profound and deep.
Seeking truth beyond the veil,
Stories of the heart unveil.

Through the whispers of the night,
We chase the glow, we seek the bright.
Every heartbeat sings a hymn,
Guiding us through realms so dim.

Reflections in a quiet stream,
Holding fragments of our dream.
In the mirror, souls ignite,
Radiant love turns dark to light.

As we wander, hope remains,
Through the trials, joy sustains.
Together, we will find our way,
To the dawn of a brand new day.

The Invitation to Awaken

Darkness fades, the dawn draws near,
In the stillness, truths appear.
Awaken now, embrace the call,
Life awaits, it's yours, it's all.

In the morning's gentle breeze,
Feel the shifts, the soul's unease.
Every moment holds a key,
Unlock the door to all you'll be.

Voices whisper, soft and clear,
Wisdom blooms, will you draw near?
Invitation painted wide,
Step into the light, let go of pride.

With each breath, the world expands,
Take a leap, make your own plans.
Awaken to the life ahead,
Dance in joy, let fear be shed.

Echoes of the Unseen

Whispers dance in shadows' embrace,
Secrets linger, lost in space.
Every echo tells a tale,
Of dreams that fade, of hope's frail sail.

In the quiet, feelings bloom,
Voices call from hidden gloom.
The unseen paths we tread along,
Carry the echoes of our song.

Time unwinds the fragile thread,
As thoughts like petals drift and spread.
In every silence, we confide,
The echoes of what dreams reside.

Yet in shadows, light can find,
The hidden truths within the blind.
What once was lost can yet be seen,
In echoes soft, where hearts convene.

In Pursuit of Passion's Light

Chasing stars through endless night,
Yearning hearts ignite with light.
Every moment fuels the fire,
In pursuit of our desire.

With open arms, we greet the dawn,
In every breath, a new dream drawn.
The path is wild, but we embrace,
The journey's thrill, the heart's sweet race.

Through valleys low and mountains high,
With courage born, we touch the sky.
In every trial, our spirits soar,
In pursuit of passion, forevermore.

Together bound, through thick and thin,
The light of love, our guiding kin.
With every step, we boldly fight,
In pursuit of passion's radiant light.

Where the Spirit Leads

Upon the winds, our souls take flight,
As hearts align with stars so bright.
In whispered dreams, we find our way,
Where spirit guides, we dare to stay.

Through forests deep and rivers wide,
With faith in tow, we choose to ride.
In every turn, in every chance,
Life unfolds its mystic dance.

In shadows cast, the light breaks through,
A journey rich with vibrant hue.
With every step, a story we weave,
Where spirit leads, we dare believe.

Embracing all that life may send,
With open hearts, we shall transcend.
For in the flow, we find our peace,
Where the spirit leads, our joys increase.

Heartstrings in the Wind

As gentle breezes start to play,
They weave our dreams in soft ballet.
Heartstrings hum a tender tune,
In every note, a wish to croon.

The world becomes a canvas wide,
With colors bright, where hearts collide.
Each whispered word, a spark divine,
Our spirits soar, our hopes align.

In storms and sunlight, we stand tall,
With every rise, we learn to fall.
For heartstrings strum a song of grace,
In wind's sweet embrace, we find our place.

So let us dance with fate's soft hands,
As love extends, and laughter stands.
For in the wind, our dreams will spin,
In heartstrings' song, the life begins.

The Call of Deeper Dreams

In shadows where the whispers play,
A world unfolds in shades of gray.
Each thought a spark, a cosmic stream,
Awakening the heart's deep dream.

With every breath, a story spins,
Of lost desires, where hope begins.
An echo stirs the silent night,
Illuminating paths with light.

Beyond the veil of what we know,
A chance to seek, to rise, to grow.
The call of dreams, both fierce and clear,
Invites the soul to venture near.

So let us dance on starlit beams,
And chase the flight of deeper dreams.
With open hearts and fearless minds,
Together, all our truth, we'll find.

Beyond the Horizon's Embrace

The sky unfurls a canvas wide,
Where hopes and wishes gently glide.
Beneath the sun's warm, golden rays,
Life stretches forth in vibrant plays.

The ocean sings a timeless song,
Inviting souls to drift along.
In every wave, in every crest,
Lies a longing to find our rest.

Beyond horizons, dreams await,
An open door, a guiding fate.
With courage deep, we'll face the tide,
Embracing all that waits inside.

Together we shall sail the sea,
In search of what is yet to be.
With hearts aligned, we'll chart the course,
For love's embrace shall be our force.

Trusting the Pulse Within

Listen closely, hear the sound,
The pulse of life, so pure, profound.
In quiet moments, truth will rise,
A whisper born from silent skies.

Trust the rhythm, follow through,
Each heartbeat echoes who is true.
In shadows deep, let courage be,
The guiding light that sets us free.

With every doubt, the spirit sings,
Reminding us of sacred things.
No fear can hold what hearts can give,
In trust, we find the will to live.

So turn within, embrace the flow,
For in that space, our spirits grow.
In trusting pulse, our souls ignite,
Together, we will find the light.

The Uncharted Map of Emotions

In caverns deep, emotions dwell,
A map drawn out, a secret spell.
Each line a tale of joy and pain,
A journey through the heart's own vein.

With every tear, a river flows,
In valleys wide, the heart still grows.
Fear not the twists, nor sudden bends,
For in each turn, the journey blends.

Discover paths of love and loss,
The weight of choices, every cross.
In laughter bright, in sorrow's sigh,
The uncharted calls, we must comply.

So take this map, make it your guide,
Through storms and calm, we will abide.
In emotions' depths, we find our glow,
A treasure trove of all we know.

Dreams on a Silver Thread

In the night, whispers play,
Silken visions drift away.
Stars collide in gentle grace,
Hope is found in time and space.

A tapestry of light unfolds,
Secrets shared, the heart beholds.
Each thread spun with daring dreams,
Weaving tales in moonlit beams.

Colors bleed, they intertwine,
Dancing shadows, soft divine.
Chasing dreams on silver streams,
Life awakens in our schemes.

Awake, we find the morning bright,
In each heart, a glowing light.
Guided by the threads we weave,
In our dreams, we learn to believe.

Beneath the Beacon's Glow

Waves crash gently on the shore,
A lighthouse stands, forevermore.
Guiding ships through darkest night,
Beneath its beam, we feel the light.

Whispers of the ocean's breeze,
Secrets dance among the trees.
Each moment flickers in the tide,
Beneath the glow, dreams confide.

Stars above like scattered gems,
Nature sings her sacred hymns.
Hearts entwined in soft embrace,
Guided home from every place.

Safe we wander, hand in hand,
With hope's promise, we will stand.
Beneath the beacon's steadfast shine,
Love illuminates, pure and divine.

Map of Inner Truths

In the stillness of the mind,
A hidden map, the heart will find.
Paths of wisdom, trails of gold,
Unravel stories yet untold.

Through valleys deep and mountains high,
We seek the truths that never die.
Each compass point, a choice to make,
An odyssey for our own sake.

Cartography of dreams and fears,
Guided by the songs of years.
In every line, a chance to grow,
A map revealing all we know.

With ink of hope, we draw our fate,
Creating paths, we navigate.
A journey blooms from deep within,
A treasured quest, let us begin.

Steps to the Silent Song

In quiet moments, shadows play,
A melody in soft display.
Each step a whisper, gentle sound,
In silence deep, our lives abound.

The rhythm of the heart unfolds,
In tranquil tones, a truth it holds.
We dance upon a whispered breeze,
The silent song brings us to ease.

With every footfall, peace is found,
A world transformed without a sound.
In echoes soft, the spirit sings,
Steps to joy, the heart takes wing.

Together we embrace the night,
In stillness, we are bathed in light.
With each soft note, we rise and soar,
Steps to the song forevermore.

Streams of Hope

In the valley where shadows lie,
Gentle waters whisper a sigh.
Bright sunbeams break through the gray,
Washing doubts of yesterday.

Each droplet tells a tale of grace,
Guiding hearts to a safer place.
Where dreams are born, and fears release,
Finding solace, finding peace.

Along the banks, flowers bloom wide,
In their colors, we will abide.
Nature's hand paints every hue,
Reminders of what hope can do.

So let us walk by the flowing stream,
And hold on tight to every dream.
With hope as our guiding light,
We'll find our way through the night.

Serendipity's Dance

In a world where paths collide,
Unexpected joys do abide.
Two souls meet, a fleeting glance,
In the moment, love's sweet dance.

With laughter echoing through the air,
Serendipity shows us care.
Footsteps tread on fateful ground,
In the warmth, pure magic found.

Stars align in cosmic play,
Guiding hearts along the way.
Spinning dreams in radiant light,
Joining two on this wondrous flight.

As the music softly plays,
Together we will weave our days.
In life's grand, surprising chance,
We dance forever, lost in trance.

The Garden of Yearning

In a garden where wishes bloom,
Whispers linger, dispelling gloom.
Petals sigh with secrets kept,
In their beauty, we have wept.

Trees stand tall with stories vast,
Roots entwined with memories past.
Breezes carry dreams untold,
As hearts unfold their dreams of gold.

In twilight's glow, shadows play,
Longing lingers at close of day.
Every flower, a hope reborn,
In the silence, souls are worn.

So walk with me through this space,
Where yearning finds a warm embrace.
In the garden, beneath the stars,
We'll cultivate our love, on Mars.

Heartstrings and Highways

On a road where freedom calls,
Echoes dance through wooden halls.
Wheels whisper tales of the whole,
As heartstrings pull at every soul.

Through valleys deep and mountains high,
Underneath the open sky.
Every mile, a story new,
Where the heart leads, dreams come true.

Adventures wait on winding bends,
With laughter shared, as travel friends.
In every turn, a song to sing,
A journey rich with everything.

So let's embrace this winding ride,
With heartstrings tied, let joy decide.
Together we'll chase the light,
In highways wide, our spirits bright.

Sailing on Wind of Dreams

Upon the crest of waves we glide,
Lost in the whispers of the tide.
Stars above like lanterns glow,
Guiding hearts where dreams can flow.

With sails of hopes and winds of fate,
We chart the course, we navigate.
Each gust a chance to rise and soar,
To places unseen, we explore.

In every ripple, secrets lie,
Adventures beckon as we fly.
Through misty seas our spirits roam,
In worlds unknown, we find our home.

So let us sail on endless skies,
And chase the dawn as daylight flies.
For in this journey, wild and bright,
We find ourselves in dreams of light.

The Allure of Possibility

In the hush of dawn, we wait,
For dreams to embolden, not vacate.
Each choice a path beneath the sun,
The dance of what could soon be done.

With open hearts, we seek and find,
A treasure trove for curious minds.
Every moment, ripe with chance,
Invites us to a daring dance.

The mountains high, the valleys deep,
Whisper secrets, ours to keep.
A canvas blank, vast as the sea,
Calls forth the realms of what might be.

So chase the spark that lights the way,
Embrace the night, welcome the day.
For in the journey, we shall see,
The endless grace of possibility.

A Vessel for Inner Whispers

In silence deep, where thoughts reside,
Our inner voices seek to guide.
With gentle nudges, they unfold,
The stories long since left untold.

Within our hearts, a vessel waits,
To hold the dreams that fate creates.
As whispers weave through time and space,
We find our truth, our sacred place.

Each moment shared, each breath we take,
Reflects the bonds that we must make.
In every laugh, in every tear,
The canvas of our lives is clear.

So let us listen, deeply hear,
The subtle call, our purpose near.
For in this vessel, we shall sail,
Through inner storms, we'll prevail.

Finding Threads of Light

Beneath the clouds where shadows creep,
A glimmer shines for us to keep.
In darkest nights, so cold and bare,
We seek the threads that lead us there.

Each sparkle small, a guiding spark,
Illuminates the paths through dark.
With open eyes, we thread the needle,
Stitching joy where fears wane, and steeple.

Through tangled woods, through winding streams,
We chase the echoes of our dreams.
For in each step, the light will grow,
Revealing truths we long to know.

So let us wander, hand in hand,
Finding the light in every land.
For in the journey, love ignites,
A tapestry of hope, our sights.

Voices from the Inner Sanctuary

In whispers soft, the thoughts arise,
A symphony of souls, 'neath starry skies.
Echoes dance in shadows of the mind,
Each note a secret, tenderly designed.

The heartbeats pulse, a rhythmic flow,
Unveiling truths we yearn to know.
Within this space where silence reigns,
The essence of our spirit remains.

A gentle breeze, the soul takes flight,
Embracing fears, igniting light.
Voices linger, as time suspends,
In this sanctuary, all hearts mend.

With every word, a bond is formed,
In sacred whispers, love is warmed.
Through inner halls, we find our grace,
In the sanctuary, we embrace.

Timeless Pursuits

Chasing dreams on endless roads,
Through fields of gold, where time erodes.
Moments forge like fire from stone,
In the dance of life, we are not alone.

Echoes of laughter, minds set free,
As we stumble through uncertainty.
With every step, a story sewn,
In timeless pursuits, our hearts have grown.

Waves crash softly on shores of fate,
In the tapestry of love, we await.
Every sunrise brings hope anew,
In the quest for dreams, we find what's true.

Through valleys deep and mountains high,
We chase the stars that light the sky.
In pursuit of joy, we learn to see,
The beauty lies in what will be.

The Lantern Within

In shadows deep, a flicker glows,
A lantern bright, where wisdom flows.
Guiding hearts through darkest nights,
In its warmth, we find our lights.

The whispers call, the spirit sings,
Illuminating all hidden things.
With each step forward, courage found,
The path unfolds on sacred ground.

Through trials faced, the lantern's beam,
Beckons hope, igniting dreams.
In every heart, a flame resides,
A beacon strong, that never hides.

As we journey through life's embrace,
The lantern shines, a guiding grace.
In the depths of self, we learn to roam,
For within us all lies a home.

Tracing the Lines of Love

In gentle strokes, a story told,
Lines of love, both soft and bold.
Every glance, a universe spun,
In the heart's embrace, two become one.

With every touch, the canvas grows,
Colors blend where passion flows.
Tracing paths where souls collide,
In the dance of love, we cannot hide.

Through the storms and brightest days,
The lines remain, despite the haze.
With every laugh, every tear shed,
The map of love is gently spread.

In the tapestry we weave each hour,
Love blooms brightly, a fragrant flower.
Tracing the lines, forever free,
In love's embrace, we find our key.

Milton Keynes UK
Ingram Content Group UK Ltd.
UKHW022209221024
449899UK00006B/38

9 789916 880388